POSTCARD HISTORY SERIES

Lighthouses and Lifesaving on the Great Lakes

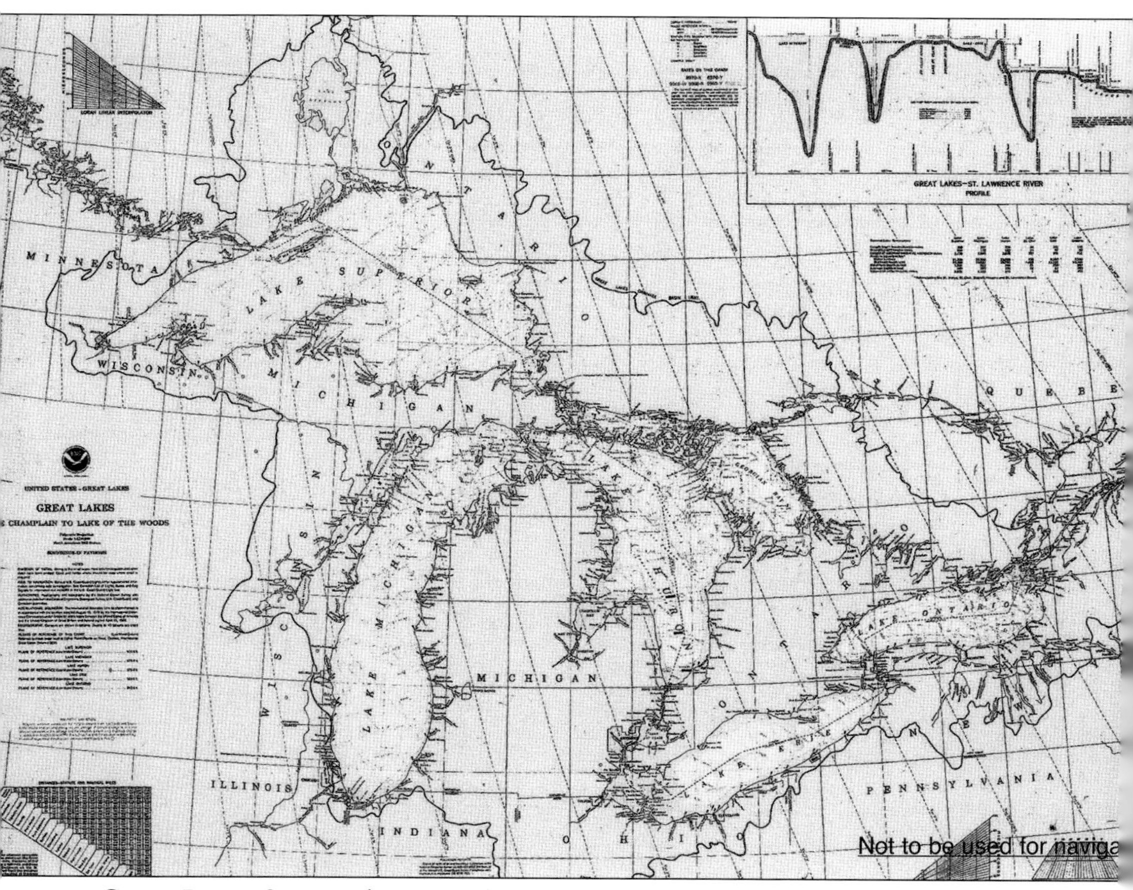

Great Lakes Chart. The Great Lakes cover 94,680 square miles and contain 5,475 cubic miles of water, enough to fill more than six quadrillion one-gallon containers. (Author's collection.)

On the Front Cover: Gross Point Light Station. The Gross Point Light Station was built on a 25-foot bluff overlooking Lake Michigan in Evanston, Illinois, in 1873. There was a tower, office, passageway, and keeper's dwelling. Two fog signal buildings were added to the station in 1880. (Author's collection.)

On the Back Cover: Ontonagon Lighthouse. The Ontonagon Lighthouse on Lake Superior in Ontonagon, Michigan, was built in 1866. It was considered a "welcoming light," meaning it was not there to warn of hazards but to aid ships on Lake Superior in finding the harbor safely. (Author's collection.)

POSTCARD HISTORY SERIES

Lighthouses and Lifesaving on the Great Lakes

Linda Osborne Cynowa

Copyright © 2022 by Linda Osborne Cynowa
ISBN 978-1-4671-0826-3

Published by Arcadia Publishing
Charleston, South Carolina

Printed in the United States of America

Library of Congress Control Number: 2022932529

For all general information contact Arcadia Publishing at:
Telephone 843-853-2070
Fax 843-853-0044
E-mail sales@arcadiapublishing.com
For customer service and orders:
Toll-Free 1-888-313-2665

Visit us on the Internet at www.arcadiapublishing.com

This book is dedicated to all the historians and archivists who work so hard to keep the many pieces of our past safe for future generations, to the many lightkeepers, both men and women, who maintained the lights in lonely conditions and helped keep the lakes as safe as possible for navigation, and to the United States Coast Guard who put their own lives in danger to rescue and aid navigation on all the Great Lakes of yesterday and today.

Contents

Acknowledgments		6
Introduction		7
1.	Lake Michigan Lights	9
2.	Lake Huron Lights	45
3.	Straits of Mackinac	57
4.	Lake Superior Lights	65
5.	Lake Erie Lights	85
6.	Lake Ontario Lights	99
7.	Lifesaving Stations	115
Resources		127

ACKNOWLEDGMENTS

It is with the greatest appreciation that I once again thank Julie Oparka, certified archivist at the Romeo District Library and Community Archives, for always supporting these projects and making the pathways easier. I also want to thank Stacie Guzzo, branch manager and archivist for the Romeo District Library. I also wish to mention and thank the many places where information was attained: the Great Lakes Lighthouse Keepers Association (GLLKA); Gulliver Historical Society; Racine Lighthouse and Maritime Preservation Society (RLAMPS); Sable Points Lighthouse Keepers Association; North Point Lighthouse Keepers Friends; the Friends of Point Betsie Lighthouse; the Gulliver Historical Society; Holland Harbor Lighthouse Historical Committee; Grassy Island Range Lights Inc.; Grand Traverse Lighthouse Foundation; Alcona Historical Society; Marblehead Lighthouse Historical Society; Kenosha County Historical Society; Delta County Historical Society; Grosse Point Light Station; City of Evanston, Illinois; Michigan Maritime Museum in South Haven; National Park Service; Manistee County Historical Museum; Michigan City Old Lighthouse Museum; Presque Isle Lighthouse Historical Society; Sanilac County Historical Society; Friends of Fort Gratiot Light; Tawas Lighthouse Friends; Presque Isle Township Museum Society; Port aux Barques Lighthouse Society; Alcona Historical Society; Emmet County; Round Island Lighthouse Society; Ontonagon County Historical Society; Minnesota Historical Society; Keweenaw County Historical Society; Crisp Point Light Historical Society; Great Lakes Shipwreck Society; Cook County Historical Society; Grand Island East Channel Light Rescue Project; Ashtabula Historical Society; Keepers of the Erie Lights; Fairport Harbor Historical Society; Dunkirk Historical Lighthouse Museum, Tibbetts Point Lighthouse Society; and Sodus Point Historical Society.

It is with great appreciation after a chance meeting that I thank Don Bauman for use of postcards from his Sturgeon Point Light collection, Jacob W. Frank Photography for his use of his Menagerie Island Light image, and Brittany Cynowa for her research abilities, historical interest, and always keeping me on the right path.

All postcards used, unless otherwise credited, are the property of the author. Any images credited as USCG are courtesy of the US Coast Guard.

Introduction

What is a lighthouse?

A lighthouse is loosely defined as a tower or structure used to display a light for the guidance of ships to either avoid a dangerous area such as shoals or reefs, or to identify a safe harbor. The purpose of the lighthouse's light is to provide ships at sea with a fixed point of reference to aid their ability to navigate in the dark when the shore or offshore hazards cannot be seen directly. The distance at which a light can be seen depends on the height and intensity of the light. The brighter the light and the greater its height above the water, the farther it can be seen.

The French physicist Augustin Jean Fresnel was born in Normandy in 1788. After an education at various institutes, his research in optics began in 1814 when he prepared a paper on the aberration of light. Fresnel's work on interference did a great deal to establish the wave theory of light. He applied mathematical analysis to his work that removed a number of objections to wave theory. He was a pioneer in the use of compound lenses instead of mirrors for lighthouses. Fresnel perfected a lens design that refracted the light from a single source into a strong directional beam essential in all modern lighthouses. Augustin Fresnel died near Paris in 1827, but his life's work did much to help shipping and navigation.

There are many stories in lighthouse and lifesaving history, like the one regarding the large rock in front of the Seul Choix Point Lighthouse, that have special meaning. Unbeknownst to their parents, a few local children built a boat-like raft to sail to Beaver Island. A storm came up, and broken pieces of the boat were discovered on the mainland. Funeral services were held for the children, who were presumed drowned, and their names were carved into the huge stone rock in front of the lighthouse. A few weeks later, Indians who had rescued the children from Gull Island returned them to their homes. The remains of Ottawa and Chippewa villages along the beaches, old foundations, and rock paintings show the early claims to the area.

Harriett Colfax served as the keeper of the Michigan City Lighthouse for 43 years, from her appointment in 1861 until her retirement at age 80 in 1904. A native of Ogdensburg, New York, she came to the area with her brother and helped with his newspaper as a typesetter. When her brother sold the paper, her cousin Schuyler Colfax, a US representative and former vice president, suggested the lighthouse of the little port in which she lived as a way of earning her living. She assumed control of the lighthouse and the old harbor beacon in the spring of 1861. Each evening during the navigational season for 43 years, she replaced the warning lamp with a fresh one; at dawn, she quenched the beacon with the knowledge that the unfailing light brought safety to many ships and small boats in the rough waters of Lake Michigan. The oldest, staunchest, and most reliable lighthouse keeper in the United States was a woman of more than 80 years of age who broke the records of all lighthouse keepers in the country in length of service, age, and above all the fact that her light never failed, never went out between the hours of sunset and sunrise during the 43 years that she tended it. Harriett Colfax passed away within a year of leaving her position in 1905.

Peter L. Shook was appointed the first keeper at the Point aux Barques light in Port Hope, Michigan, on Lake Huron in 1848, but while sailing to Port Huron in March 1849, his boat capsized, and he and his three companions drowned. Shook was 40 years old at the time and left a wife and eight children. Catherine Shook was appointed keeper in her husband's place, becoming Michigan's first female light keeper. Shortly after her husband's death, a fire broke out in the keeper's dwelling. The report stated, "The circumstances of this fire is the more to be regrettable and with double severity upon the widow who was lately appointed in his place. By this catastrophe, the widow not only lost a considerable amount of her furniture, but was badly burned in her attempt to keep the fire from the main building. They have erected temporarily a small shanty for her family, so there is hope that no time will be lost in having the dwelling rebuilt." Catherine performed her duties very well, though the strain of keeping the light and caring for her children may have been too much, as she resigned her position in March 1851. She passed away nine years later and was buried next to her husband in Oakwood Cemetery in New Baltimore, Michigan.

The Great Lakes Storm of 1913 was the deadliest, most destructive natural disaster in recorded history to hit the lakes. It killed more than 250 people, destroyed 19 ships, and stranded 19 others. As much as $1 million of cargo, including coal, iron ore, and grain weighing as much as 68,300 tons was lost. Winds reached 90 miles per hour and stirred up waves as high as 35 feet with whiteout conditions. Called the "White Hurricane," this storm became a blizzard with hurricane-force winds that devastated the Great Lakes, the midwestern United States, and southwestern Ontario from November 7 to 10, 1913.

The keepers learned to live with danger every day. Tragedy struck the Spectacle Reef Lighthouse in April 1883 when head keeper William A. Marshall departed in a boat for the lighthouse to open it for the season. With him was his son James Marshall, who was the second acting assistant keeper; William's brother Walter Marshall, the newly appointed third assistant keeper; and Edward Chambers, the first assistant keeper. Along for the ride were friends of James Marshall, 16-year-old Joseph Cardran and his brother, 13-year-old Alfred Cardran. It is not known if they were in two boats or just one. At some point, their boat capsized when a gust of wind struck as the men were adjusting the sails, throwing all of them into the icy water. The Cardran brothers, being young and excellent swimmers, assisted William and Walter, who could not swim, to safety with difficulty. Joseph Cardran dove into the water once again and rescued Edward Chambers. James Marshall was not found and was believed drowned. Unfortunately, they had to petition Congress for reimbursement for their personal effects that had been lost. When Joseph Cardran turned 18, he joined the US Lighthouse Service as a third assistant keeper but resigned after just seven months. Five years later in 1889, Alfred Cardran also joined the service as a third assistant keeper at Spectacle Reef, but he also eventually resigned. The isolation of some of the reef lights was more than many could handle.

The US Revenue Cutter Service was created by Congress on August 4, 1790, at the request of Alexander Hamilton as the Revenue-Marine; it is the oldest continuous seagoing service of the United States. The United States Life-Saving Service (USLSS) was formed to address safety issues on the Great Lakes. With a growing shipping business came an increase in accidents.

One

Lake Michigan Lights

Manitowoc Lighthouse, Wisconsin. Native Americans call this bay in Lake Michigan Manitowoc, meaning "home of the great spirit," because of its natural beauty. Construction of a lighthouse at Manitowoc began in 1837. After land was purchased on high ground near the mouth of the Manitowoc River, work began on a brick tower that tapered from a diameter of 12 feet at its base to 6.5 feet for the lantern room. The tower measured 30 feet tall from the base to the ventilator ball. The keeper's house was a 1.5-story detached brick building. The tower became obsolete in 1877; a pier light was deemed more sufficient for the harbor by then. This image is from around 1907.

WIND POINT LIGHTHOUSE, RACINE, WISCONSIN. Construction began on a light and fog signal at Racine Point in 1877. Its 108-foot conical tower was placed on a dressed limestone foundation. Built of brick with an inner and outer wall, the Wind Point Lighthouse gradually tapers from a diameter of 22 feet at the base to 12 feet, 8 inches at the lantern. The revolving lens could be seen for up to 16 miles. The tower has two distinctive architectural embellishments seen in many of the tall towers on the Great Lakes—masonry gallery-support corbels and arch-topped windows. The 1.5-story brick keeper's house was attached to the tower by an enclosed passage. In 1997, ownership of the complex was transferred to the Village of Wind Point, while the Coast Guard maintained the light. The image at left is from around 1916, and one below is from around 1941.

White River Light Station, Whitehall, Michigan. Construction of the main lighthouse where Lake Michigan and the White River meet began in 1875, and both the tower and the light keeper's 1.5-story house had foundations of dressed limestone blocks. The 38-foot tower was set into the northwest corner of the house and covered with limestone bricks. Open grillwork iron stairs spiraled from the basement up to the lantern with a fourth-order Fresnel lens. By 1918, the lighthouse was converted to electricity. As the timber industry faded out, the White Lake area became popular as a tourist destination. The White River Lighthouse was deactivated in 1960 and turned over to the General Service Administration. Fruitland Township later purchased the property for use of a museum and public park. The station is pictured above around 1952 and below around 1905.

NORTH POINT LIGHTHOUSE, MILWAUKEE, WISCONSIN. In 1852, this Milwaukee lighthouse was relocated, as the first one was not ideal for shipping concerns. In 1868, the tower was raised four feet and equipped with a new lantern and fourth-order Fresnel lens. In 1886, a new station was built at the western boundary of the lighthouse lot. The keeper's house was built in the Queen Anne style and attached to the tower by an enclosed passage. The city developed Lake Park around the lighthouse and allowed a carriage road and two bridges to be built just east of the light, with sculpted sandstone lions to guard each end of the bridge. The old tower was set on top of the new steel tower in July 1912 in the same octagonal shape. The light was electrified in 1943 but soon became obsolete, and the light was discontinued in 1994. The above image shows the lighthouse around 1911; below, it is seen around 1907.

MISSION POINT LIGHTHOUSE, TRAVERSE CITY, MICHIGAN. In 1859, Congress decided to place a lighthouse on the end of the peninsula known as Old Mission Point, but with the Civil War, it was 1869 before a schoolhouse style lighthouse was built. The 1.5-story keeper's cottage measured 30 by 28 feet and had a 36-foot tower. Its fifth-order Fresnel lens could be seen for 13 miles. In 1889, a 200-foot timber and rock breakwater was built in front of the lighthouse to prevent erosion. When an automated light was built offshore right on the underwater shoals in 1938, the Old Mission Point light was deactivated. Residents of Peninsular Township raised funds to purchase the lighthouse and property in 1948 to add to their new park. The above image was taken before 1907.

Little Sable Point Lighthouse, Mears, Michigan. Construction of the 115-foot tower and 2.5-story brick dwelling was completed in the spring of 1879. A lens made of hand-ground glass prisms intensified the light so it could be seen for 19 miles out into the lake. In order to make the tower more visible as a daymark, it was painted white in May 1899. In 1910, the name of the lighthouse changed from Petite Point au Sable, French for "Little Point of Sand," to Little Sable Point Light Station. In 1915, the light was changed to an incandescent oil vapor lamp, which produced a brighter light. To reduce maintenance, the Coast Guard removed the white paint from the tower in 1976.

POINT BETSIE LIGHTHOUSE, FRANKFORT, MICHIGAN. Originally named Bec Scies, the area became known as Point Betsie when the lighthouse was built at the opening of the Manitou Passage in 1858. The yellow brick lighthouse had a circular 37-foot tower with a fourth-order Fresnel lens and a passageway that connected to the two-story keeper's house. Within a year, sand erosion around the light made it necessary to put a large concrete apron around it, and a stone and timber breakwater was also built at the edge of the water to take the brunt of the wave action. In 1900, the tower and keeper's house had a new look; it was painted white and a bright red roof was added for better visibility. It was one of the last lights on the Great Lakes to be automated, in 1983.

LITTLE TRAVERSE LIGHTHOUSE, HARBOR SPRINGS, MICHIGAN. In early 1884, a parcel of land was acquired on Harbor Point in Harbor Springs at the entrance of Little Traverse Bay. The redbrick 1.5-story keeper's house had a 40-foot high tower attached to the south side, where the tower was integrated as part of the house and gable. In 1896, a two-story, square, pyramidal, fog bell tower was erected. The bell was struck a double blow every 30 seconds when needed. In 1914, the fog bell was changed to a single blow every 15 seconds. A brick oil house was built to store the kerosene that was used at that time. In 1963, when the light was automated, it closed for operation. It is now in private hands and is often called Harbor Point Light.

Big Sable Point Lighthouse, Ludington, Michigan. Nine miles north of Ludington, the 112-foot tower and decagonal lantern with a third-order Fresnel lens was first lit in 1867 and was visible for 20 miles. The original 1.5-story Cape Cod–style keeper's house was built in Milwaukee cream city brick and painted white when completed. A passageway where the keeper's office was located connected the tower to the keeper's house. By the 1890s, the soft yellow brick was crumbling near the tower base. It was encased in 18 metal cylinders, each one slightly small in order for them to fit into one another, then concrete poured between the cylinders and original brick. In 1910, the name was changed to Big Sable Point. Until a road was built in the 1930s, the light was only accessible by water.

FRANKFORT NORTH BREAKWATER LIGHT, FRANKFORT, MICHIGAN, C. 1947. In 1912, funds were appropriated to build a taller light at the end of the north pier at the harbor entrance. The tower has a height of 44 feet and was painted white to make the most of visibility. The tower, covered in steel plating, has a square gallery that holds a decagonal lantern with a fourth-order Fresnel lens. The red fixed light could be seen for 12 miles. The tower was connected to the main shoreline by an elevated catwalk. The light was electrified in 1919. As with most pier lights, this beacon was relocated numerous times as the pier was extended. Winter winds and freezing water made for very treacherous trips to the light tower for the light keepers during the winter months on Lake Michigan.

Seul Choix Point Lighthouse, Gulliver, Michigan, c. 1938. Seul Choix Point (pronounced "Sis Shwa") was named by North American Indians and French traders who found the protected bays their "only choice" for shelter along this stretch of northern Michigan shoreline. It turned out to be the only place along Lake Michigan's north shore for 100 miles to offer protection between the St. Helena lighthouse in the Straits of Mackinac and the Poverty Island Light. The tower and attached 1.5-story keeper's dwelling, steam-powered fog signal building, outbuildings, two docks, and a tram for carrying supplies to the complex were finished in 1895. The station's last keeper left in 1972 when the light was automated and the third-order Fresnel lens was removed. The Gulliver Historical Society was formed in 1987 and opened a museum on the grounds.

CANA ISLAND LIGHTHOUSE, BAILEY'S HARBOR, WISCONSIN. At the top of the 89-foot tower, the Cana Island light affords a beautiful view of the coastline of the Door County peninsula. The light is northeast of Bailey's Harbor on a peninsula between North Bay and Moonlight Bay on the nine-acre island. A 300-foot causeway links the island to the mainland. The lighthouse was built in 1869 of Milwaukee cream city yellow brick, for both the tower and the 1.5-story keeper's house. In 1902, the tower was encased in iron bands with the space between filled with concrete to prevent further erosion. With its original third-order Fresnel lens, it has a visibility of 18 miles. In 1941, the light was automated. Since 1970, the Door County Maritime Museum has been an integral part of the preservation of the lighthouse.

EAGLE BLUFF LIGHTHOUSE, EPHRAIM, DOOR COUNTY, WISCONSIN. In 1866, a lighthouse was built on Eagle Bluff, three miles north of Fish Creek, in the narrow shipping passage between the Door County peninsula and Strawberry Island. Built with cream-colored Milwaukee brick, the keeper's house measured 26 by 30 feet, with an attached wing. The attached 43-foot light tower housed a three-and-a-half-order Fresnel lens with a visibility of 16 miles. The light was converted to an unmanned acetylene light in 1926. The Coast Guard replaced the acetylene gas system with a battery-powered light, and the lantern room now had a fifth-order Fresnel lens, having been changed in 1918. Since 2003, the Door County Historical Society keeps watch over this much visited lighthouse. (Both, courtesy of Terry Pepper and GLLKA.)

HOLLAND HARBOR LIGHTHOUSE, HOLLAND, MICHIGAN. In 1870, the government appropriated funds to build a pierhead light at the end of the south pier for the harbor entrance. The light was a 27-foot white pyramidal beacon with its upper portion enclosed in clapboard and the lower level left open for waves to wash through. The polygonal lantern housed a fifth-order Fresnel lens that had a 32-foot focal plane with a visibility of 11.5 miles. By 1902, a steel tower replaced the deteriorating wooden tower. The wooden catwalk was replaced with a steel one. The buff-colored lighthouse was given a new coat of red paint in 1956, and it became known as "Big Red" with its distinctive daymark. In 1970, the light was automated and the fog signal moved. Now, the Holland Harbor Lighthouse Historical Committee maintains the light. These images are from around 1913.

GRASSY ISLAND RANGE LIGHTS, GREEN BAY, WISCONSIN. Both of the range lights were tapering towers covered in cedar shake shingles. The northern front tower was 25 feet with an octagonal cast-iron lantern with a sixth-order Fresnel lens, displaying a fixed white light with an 11-mile range. The southern rear tower was 35 feet with an octagonal lantern with a sixth-order Fresnel lens and a 13-mile range. A 2.5-story keeper's house was built, and the lights were lit in 1872. The weather and water condition made upgrades a continuous problem. By 1934, the fixed white lights were changed to green to make them more visible. By 1998, the lights were relocated to the breakwall on the west side of the harbor. These images are from around 1908.

GRAND TRAVERSE LIGHTHOUSE, NORTHPORT, LEELANAU COUNTY, MICHIGAN. Originally called the Cat Head Lighthouse, Grand Traverse sits at the end of the Leelanau Peninsula, marking the entrance to the Manitou Passage and the Straits of Mackinac. In 1858, the first lighthouse to serve the area was torn down. A 2.5-story, 30-by-32-foot keeper's house was built in its place using Milwaukee cream city brick. It was given a slate roof, with a seven-foot wooden tower placed on the gable end. In 1870, the fifth-order Fresnel lens was exchanged for the more powerful fourth-order Barbier and Finestre lens. The light was electrified in 1950, and by 1972, keepers and caretakers were no longer needed. By 2003, ownership was transferred from the Coast Guard to the Michigan Department of Parks and Recreation.

ST. JAMES HARBOR LIGHTHOUSE AND BEAVER HEAD LIGHTHOUSE, ST JAMES, MICHIGAN. Above, the St. James Harbor light was built in 1856. Because of poor construction, it needed to be rebuilt in 1870. The lighthouse sat at the northeast end of Beaver Island at the north side of the harbor entrance to Paradise Bay. At right, Beaver Head Lighthouse is on the south end of Beaver Island on a high bluff above Lake Michigan. Constructed in 1851 with building materials of a mediocre nature, a new tower was needed by 1858. The new 46-foot yellow brick conical tower had a lantern room that housed a fourth-order Fresnel lens. It had a visibility of 18 miles. By 1866, a yellow brick keeper's house was added, with a covered passageway to connect the house with the tower. In 1962, the Coast Guard replaced the light with an automated radio beacon tower.

South Manitou Island Lighthouse, Glen Arbor Township, Michigan. In 1840, the first of three lights at this location was a rubble stone 1.5-story keeper's house with a short wooden tower on top of the house. By 1857, the second lighthouse was built after the deterioration of the original, this being built with yellow brick, again with a short wooden tower and lantern room using a fourth-order Fresnel lens. The double-layer conical redbrick tower had an 18-foot base and housed a third-order Fresnel lens. The tower was painted white with black trim for the best visibility. A 40-foot-long covered passage was attached to the 1858 keeper's house. South Manitou Island Lighthouse was deactivated in 1958 and became part of the Sleeping Bear Dunes National Lakeshore in 1970.

STURGEON BAY SHIP CANAL LIGHTHOUSE, STURGEON BAY, WISCONSIN. In 1881, the Sturgeon Bay pierhead light was built on the end of the pier. As traffic increased through the canal, by 1890, a coastal light was erected onshore near the keeper's house for the pinhead light. On a concrete foundation, a double-walled, steel, eight-foot cylinder was erected to a height of 98 feet with a circular lantern room with four portholes in the watch room. The lantern held a second-order Fresnel lens. The light was originally painted reddish brown; however, by 1900, it was painted bright white to provide a better daymark. The present skeletal framework was erected around 1899 to help with wind vibration issues in 1903. Today, it is an active Coast Guard base.

KENOSHA (SOUTHPORT) LIGHTHOUSE, KENOSHA, WISCONSIN. It was known as Southport in 1837 and Kenosha by 1850. There would be three different lighthouses over the years before a permanent lighthouse and tower were situated on the Southport site between 1847 and 1866. The third one was a 55-foot conical tower built of yellow Milwaukee brick on a stone foundation. It has a decagonal lantern room for its fourth-order Fresnel lens. Interior lighting came from three windows in the tower. The keeper's house, a separate two-story building also of yellow brick, was finished in 1867. By 1906, the light was deactivated and replaced by a pierhead one. Today, the light is only lit on special occasions. The historical society continues to work on renovations for this light to be used as a museum. (Below, courtesy of the National Archives.)

Gross Point Light Station, Evanston, Illinois. Standing on a 25-foot bluff overlooking Lake Michigan in Evanston, the Grosse Point Light Station has served navigational traffic in the Chicago area since 1873. The tower stands 113 feet tall, and was originally constructed of metal, yellow brick, and glass along with the duplex keeper's house with its red roof and trim. In 1914, after deterioration of the exterior brick, a facing of concrete was laid over it. The lantern room housed a second-order Fresnel lens, the largest type used on the Great Lakes. The light could be seen for up to 20 miles. It was electrified and automated in 1922. The station was decommissioned by the US Lighthouse Service in 1935. Restoration began in its centennial year of 1973.

SHERWOOD POINT LIGHTHOUSE, IDLEWILD, WISCONSIN. In 1883, a 1.5-story keeper's house was built of redbrick with a square light tower on the lakefront side. The tower, painted white, supported a square red gallery with a decagonal white cast-iron lantern. This lighthouse was the only light in Door County to be built of redbrick. Sherwood Point's light was a white light alternating with red and could be seen on a clear night up to 18 miles. The point was electrified in the mid 1930s, but by the 1980s, automation came to the area. At that time, Sherwood Point was the last manned lighthouse on the US side of the Great Lakes. The Coast Guard still maintains the lighthouse and property. (Above, courtesy of the USCG.)

LUDINGTON NORTH BREAKWATER LIGHTHOUSE, LUDINGTON, MICHIGAN. The year 1870 saw the first light in Ludington. A variety of lights were used until 1924, when a square, white, tapering pyramidal tower was built, rising 57 feet from the base to the ventilator. Because of the Michigan winter storms, the steel frame tower was encased in riveted steel plates. A wedge-like protrusion stood out at its base to take the force of the fierce waves that lashed the lighthouse. Its fourth-order Fresnel lens could be seen for 19 miles. In 1972, the light was automated. In 1994, the US Army Corps of Engineers discovered the base of the tower was leaning as much as four degrees, but rectifying the tilt would be prohibitive. By 1995, the Fresnel lens was dismantled and replaced with a 300-mm plastic lens with much less weight, which helped lessen the leaning of the tower.

OLD MICHIGAN CITY LIGHTHOUSE, MICHIGAN CITY, INDIANA. Michigan City is 60 miles east of Chicago on the southeast side of Lake Michigan. As the port continued to grow, a new lighthouse was built in Michigan City in 1858. The new keeper's house had a short, square wooden tower constructed on top of the northern end of the seven-room, 1.5-story building. The foundation of the building used Joliet stone, a strong type of granite, because of the blasts of sand from the dunes, with Milwaukee cream city brick on the upper portion. The lantern room had nine sides and used a fifth-order Fresnel lens. Harriett Colfax was the keeper of this light from 1861 to 1904, stopping only a year before she died at 80.

Rawley Point Lighthouse, Twin Rivers, Wisconsin. Rawley Point is on the west side of Lake Michigan about five miles north of Twin Rivers, Wisconsin. In 1873, a 2.5-story brick keeper's house with an attached tower 100 feet tall, which housed a third-order Fresnel lens, was built. By 1890, a steam fog whistle was added to the station. In 1892, the brick tower needed to be strengthened, and a skeletal tower was soon built to replace the existing one. When a new, larger and stronger light was needed, the original tower was reduced to half its height with a new hexagonal roof, and the remaining tower was redesigned into living space. The erector-style tower replaced the original brick one in 1894. By 1979, the station was automated. (Right, courtesy of the National Archives.)

MILWAUKEE HARBOR PIER LIGHT, MILWAUKEE, WISCONSIN. After the channel was dredged deeper and the pier was extended in 1868, the original white square tower with an open base was built in 1872. In 1906, the original wooden tower was replaced with the 41-foot tower made of cast-iron bands riveted together in a conical shape seen here. The circular cast-iron lantern housed a fourth-order Fresnel lens. The lens was later moved to the Breakwater light and a fifth-order lens installed.

MILWAUKEE BREAKWATER LIGHT, MILWAUKEE, WISCONSIN, C. 1911. The first harbor Breakwater light in Milwaukee was on a bluff overlooking the lake; it was deemed too far from the lake itself. In 1855, the bluff light was replaced with a taller light built north of the city, and the old light was torn down. By 1908, and for the next few years, the Milwaukee lightship was used in the area. By 1926, construction of a larger light station was completed.

South Haven South Pier Light, South Haven, Michigan. In 1861, locals built two protective piers out into the lake from the Black River. In 1871, Congress appropriated funds for the second time to build a 30-foot-tall, white wooden pyramidal tower with the top encased in clapboard and the bottom half open to the elements. In 1872, the light was first lit. The year 1902 saw a fifth-order Fresnel lens placed at the light. A replacement tower made of riveted bands of iron in a conical shape was 35 in height and painted white. It was electrified in 1923, and soon, the tower was painted red to meet new regulations. This lighthouse is one of only a few that still keeps a catwalk. Pictured above before 1907 is the SS *Eastland*, which met with tragedy in 1915.

SAND POINT LIGHTHOUSE, ESCANABA, MICHIGAN. Sand Point Lighthouse was built in 1868 to mark the harbor entrance and warn mariners of the sandy shoals at the point. The square yellow brick building, a 1.5-story keeper's house, had an attached 41-foot square brick tower, painted white for better visibility. The decagonal lantern housed a fourth-order Fresnel lens. The construction was considered unusual as the tower faced away from the water. By 1985, the light was transferred to the Delta County Historical Society.

PENINSULA POINT LIGHTHOUSE, RAPID RIVER, MICHIGAN. In 1864, a yellow brick lighthouse was built with a square 40-foot tower attached to the 1.5-story keeper's dwelling. A fourth-order Fresnel lens was installed in the decagonal lantern room. It was an important navigational aid until 1934 because of the shoals and reefs. In 1937, custodianship was given to the National Forest Service. In 1959, the house portion succumbed to a fire, and only the tower stands today. (Courtesy of the National Archives.)

LITTLE FORT LIGHTHOUSE, WAUKEGAN, ILLINOIS, C. 1890. In 1844, a lighthouse was built on a southern bluff of Lake Michigan. A small, six-room, 1.5-story brick keeper's house with an attached wooden tower on the roof was built just north of the old light. Foregoing lamps and reflectors, a fifth-order Fresnel lens was installed in 1860. The lot was fenced and the tower painted white in 1890. This light served until 1898.

WAUKEGAN HARBOR PIER LIGHTHOUSE. This pierhead light was placed to mark the entry to the harbor starting with the 1899 shipping season. After a concrete foundation was completed at the end of the south pier, a metal tower was erected and a fourth-order Fresnel lens was installed. A 400-foot-long elevated walk was built along the pier. This is a pre-1907 postcard.

KENOSHA PIERHEAD LIGHTHOUSE, KENOSHA, WISCONSIN. In 1865, a 30-foot timber framed pyramidal light with an enclosed lantern was built. With its sixth-order Fresnel lens, it had a visibility of 12 miles. Over the years, the pier was extended, with the light moved to the new end of the pier. In 1906, a new light was constructed with cast-iron rings riveted together. In 1917, the white paint was changed to red. The light was electrified in 1925.

MICHIGAN CITY EAST PIER LIGHTHOUSE, MICHIGAN CITY, INDIANA. Because of a growing need in the port city, a short square wooden tower was constructed atop a new seven-room, 1.5-story building. The foundation of the structure was built of Joliet stone, and Milwaukee cream city brick was used for the upper portion. The lantern room had nine sides and a fifth-order Fresnel lens. In 1933, the light was electrified, and by 1960, it was completely automated.

Chicago Harbor Pier Light, Chicago, Illinois. The new 48-foot conical tower had to be lined with bricks, and the keeper's quarters were attached to the tower. It had a decagonal lantern with third-order Fresnel lens. The Chicago Harbor Lighthouse keepers had three important jobs—to keep the light in working order, to activate the fog signal, and to maintain the radio beacon. The tower was automated in 1979. (Courtesy of the USCG.)

Racine Harbor Lighthouse, Racine, Wisconsin (Pre-1907 Postcard). A new 1.5-story schoolhouse-style light built of yellow brick painted white was added to the harbor entrance. A square 36-foot tower was built into the east end of this keeper's dwelling. A fifth-order Fresnel lens from the previous light was used in the new lantern room, with a 13-mile visibility. The harbor light was discontinued when a new north pierhead light was activated in 1903. It is now in private hands.

ST. JOSEPH HARBOR AND PIER LIGHTHOUSES, ST. JOSEPH, MICHIGAN. The first lighthouse on Lake Michigan was built on a bluff in St. Joseph, Michigan, in 1832. Within 14 years, a wooden pier was built extending into Lake Michigan with a new lighthouse constructed at the end of the pier and a fourth-order Fresnel lens. A steel outer light was added in 1907 using a fifth-order Fresnel lens. These range lights are still in use today.

CHARLEVOIX SOUTH PIER LIGHT STATION, CHARLEVOIX, MICHIGAN. In 1948, a new steel structure was installed on the south pier, where it was originally painted daymark red. In 1989, the present steel and concrete pier replaced the old wooden pier due to constant wave pressure. The first light was used for navigation into the Pine River channel. Its 56-foot-tall tower could be seen for 19 miles. It was in use for 63 years before deterioration made a second light necessary.

Grand Haven Bluff Lighthouse, Grand Haven, Michigan. A new lighthouse was built at the top of a bluff on the south side of the harbor. The keeper's house was constructed of stone and had a tower on the south end. It used a fourth-order Fresnel lens with a visibility of 18 miles. By 1905, as changes occurred with new pier lights, the lighthouse on the bluff was discontinued, and its fourth-order lens was moved to the rear range light.

North Manitou Shoals Light, Leelanau County, Michigan. Before the North Manitou Shoal Light was built, the hazardous shoal was protected by nearby North Manitou Island Light or a lightship. This crib light was built on the shoal in 1935 in 26 feet of water. The 63-foot tower used the fourth-order Fresnel lens that had previously been installed at the North Manitou Island light. By 1980, the light was automated, and the six revolving keepers were no longer necessary.

GREEN BAY HARBOR LIGHT, SCOTT, WISCONSIN. This light was constructed on a circular concrete pier in 1935. The round service room was also used as keeper's quarters. A small tapering tower housed a fourth-order Fresnel lens. The Coast Guard took over the care of the country's lights in 1939, and two guardsmen would serve alternating duties at the crib, two weeks on and two weeks off. When automated in 1979, there was no longer a need for keepers.

RACINE REEF LIGHT, RACINE, WISCONSIN, C. 1935. The reef outside the harbor was not lit adequately until 1906. A 60-foot-square timber crib supported an octagonal concrete pier for the basement engine room. Built in the Victorian style with an internal metal frame to cover the brick, the light had five levels and stood 66 feet tall. The lantern room housed a fourth-order Fresnel lens. The station was electrified by 1939 and automated by 1954.

Muskegon South Pierhead Light, Muskegon, Michigan. The present circular metal tower, the third light to be placed in this area, was erected near the inner end of the south pier in 1903. The circular tower, 55 feet tall and made with riveted bands of iron, used a fourth-order Fresnel lens. In 1917, the structures supporting the pierhead range lights were painted red. In 2010, the Michigan Lighthouse Conservancy became the new owners of the Muskegon South Pierhead Light.

Ashland Breakwater Light, Ashland, Wisconsin. This tower is hexagonal in plan and pyramidal in shape, with a cylindrical watch room. The walls are reinforced concrete except for the watch room, which is made of steel. The living quarters were housed on the second and third stories when needed. A pier with a derrick was used to handle the keeper's launch. The Fresnel lens was replaced by a modern optic in 1980.

MANISTEE NORTH PIER LIGHT, MANISTEE, MICHIGAN. The first light was on the south pier in 1870. It burned during the great fire of 1871. By the 1890s, navigational traffic had increased in Manistee harbor, making it necessary to place a pierhead light at the end of the north pier. The pierhead light and fog signal were transferred from the south pier to the north. By 1927, after many moves from the mainland to piers on both the north and south sides of the harbor, a light with a white cylinder constructed of cast iron was placed on the north pier with a fifth-order Fresnel lens. The tower has a 10-sided lantern room and uses a 5,000-candlepower incandescent electric bulb that is visible for 12 miles. The tower has been refurbished as the pier was extended. The present tower is 39 feet tall. The catwalk is one of only four in Michigan.

Two

Lake Huron Lights

New Presque Isle Lighthouse, Presque Isle, Michigan. The Presque Isle Light is one of a group of lights known as the "Tall Lighthouses of the Great Lakes." Others are Big Sable Light on Lake Michigan, 1867; South Manitou on Lake Michigan, 1872; Grosse Point Light on Lake Michigan, 1873; Little Sable Light on Lake Michigan, 1874; Au Sable Light on Lake Superior, 1874; and Wind Point on Lake Michigan, 1880. Orlando Metcalfe Poe was a US Army officer and engineer in the Civil War. After taking part in Gen. William Tecumseh Sherman's March to the Sea, he was responsible for much of the early lighthouse construction on the Great Lakes. These lights were built from his plans.

NEW PRESQUE ISLE LIGHTHOUSE, LAKE HURON, MICHIGAN. At 113 feet, this is the tallest lighthouse on the Great Lakes. It has four unique arched windows below the pedestal room and a large band of brick around the top of the light, just below the windows. The tower walls were built using a double-wall style; the outer brick wall was built to taper as it rose. It has a decagonal lantern room with a third-order Fresnel lens, and the light was visible for 20 miles. A 1.5-story brick keeper's house was attached to the tower with a covered passage. For good visibility, the house and tower were painted white. The light station was fully automated in 1970. Presque Isle Township took over ownership from the Coast Guard to use it as a park. In 1985, the nonprofit Presque Isle Lighthouse Historical Society was formed.

Port Sanilac Lighthouse, Port Sanilac, Michigan. Built in 1886, both the keeper's house and tower were constructed of redbrick and placed on a foundation of stone. The octagonal tower is 14 feet at the base and tapers up to nine feet. At the top of the tower, the brickwork starts a stepped pattern to support the gallery, an octagonal hourglass shape. The tower is 59 feet from the base to the ventilator ball and can be seen for up to 15 miles with its fourth-order Fresnel lens. The two-story keeper's house is attached to the tower by a covered passageway with a veranda. After the light was automated, it was sold into private ownership in 1928, with the tower remaining the responsibility of the US Coast Guard.

FORT GRATIOT LIGHT STATION, PORT HURON, MICHIGAN. In 1823, a tower 32 feet high was built. By 1828, deterioration and erosion and a collapse into the St. Clair River made it necessary to start again. In 1829, the new lighthouse, constructed of brick, stood 65 feet high with a 25-foot diameter. By 1862, the tower was increased to 82 feet and fitted with a third-order Fresnel lens with a white light. In 1874, a brick duplex keeper's house was added. By 1933, the light was fully automated and was changed to a green light with a 16-mile visibility. The site for the light station is a five-acre campus on Lake Huron where the lake and the St. Clair River meet. Today, the light is maintained by the US Coast Guard.

Tawas Point Lighthouse, East Tawas, Michigan. As early as 1850, Lake Huron was becoming a center for commerce in the Great Lakes. In 1850, the curving hook of Ottawa Point was a natural shelter for a light to be placed for use in Tawas Bay. Soon a fifth-order Fresnel lens was installed in the tower to improve navigation. Because of the natural reshaping of the point, a second light was built with a 67-foot tower and a decagonal lantern room in 1876. Now a fourth-order Fresnel lens was used with a visibility of 16 miles. Connected to the tower by a covered passageway was a redbrick, two-story keeper's house that had eight rooms for the keeper and his family. In 1922, an existing house was purchased as an assistant keeper's dwelling and moved to the station.

HARBOR BEACH LIGHTHOUSE, HARBOR BEACH, MICHIGAN. In 1885, this lighthouse was built on a timber foundation crib. It is a "spark plug" style, conical brick structure encased in cast-iron plates with an original brown color. A round cast-iron watch room has a 10-sided cast-iron lantern. The light sits 54 feet above the harbor in a 45-foot tower housing a fourth-order Fresnel lens with a visibility of 16 miles. The first floor of the lighthouse had room for a kitchen and living space. The next two floors had sleeping areas, and the fourth floor housed a workroom. The fifth floor held a watch room, and the lantern room at the top of the sixth level filled the tower space. In 1900, the tower color was changed to white.

OLD PRESQUE ISLE LIGHTHOUSE, PRESQUE ISLE, MICHIGAN, C. 1940. Presque Isle is French and translates to "almost an island." The conical tower here was 30 feet high with a base of 18 feet in diameter. The rubble-stone walls were four feet thick, and the light burned whale oil when first lit in 1840. In 1857, the light upgraded to a fourth-order Fresnel lens. There was a 1.5-story keeper's quarters, measuring 35 by 20 feet, built just north of the tower. When a new light was built in 1870, this light was abandoned after 30 years of service. The light was sold into private ownership in 1897. In 1995, the light and museum were sold to Presque Isle Township, where they continue as a museum.

FORTY MILE POINT LIGHTHOUSE, ROGERS CITY, MICHIGAN. In 1896, construction began on a rectangular, redbrick duplex with a tower rising up the middle of the lake-facing side. The 52-foot tower divided the house into two equal sections, each with its own entry. The three-story tower had double windows on its first two levels and single windows on its third. The tower housed a fourth-order Fresnel lens. The light was first lit in 1897. It was automated in 1969.

PRESQUE ISLE REAR RANGE LIGHTHOUSE, HARBOR VIEW, MICHIGAN. This light worked in tandem with a light nearer to the shore. This rear lighthouse had a tower mounted on top of the roof of the 1.5-story, five-room keeper's house. It had a focal plane 36 feet above the harbor, twice the height of the front light. It was eventually sold to private owners.

POINT AUX BARQUES LIGHTHOUSE, PORT HOPE, MICHIGAN. Although little is known about the first light at Point aux Barques, in 1857 a second lighthouse was built out of Milwaukee cream city brick with an 89-foot tower. The foundation was made of limestone and placed on a 12-foot bluff near the shore. The cast-iron lantern room holds a third-order Fresnel lens with a visibility of 16 miles. The 1.5-story brick keeper's house has a covered passageway connected to the tower. In 1875, a lifesaving station was built south of the tower. By 1957, the light was fully automated. Today, it is part of Huron County's Lighthouse Park and Ship Wreck Museum.

STURGEON POINT LIGHTHOUSE, HARRISVILLE, MICHIGAN. Built in 1869, the conical yellow brick tower was set on a limestone foundation. The base of the tower was 16 feet in diameter with walls 4.5 feet thick. At the top, the walls were 10 feet in diameter and 1.5 feet thick. The decagonal lantern room was topped by a red decagonal dome and ventilator ball, making the tower over 70 feet tall. When completed in 1869, it received a three-and-a-half-order Fresnel lens, which gave it a 16-mile visibility. The brick keeper's house had an 11-foot covered passageway connecting to the tower. Both the tower and keeper's house were painted white for ease of visibility. In 1876, the Sturgeon Bay Life Saving Station was added to the point. (Both, courtesy of Don Bauman.)

MIDDLE ISLAND LIGHTHOUSE, ALPENA, MICHIGAN. This 71-foot conical tower was 21 feet in diameter at the base with two-foot thick walls when built in 1904. The decagonal cast-iron lantern housed a fourth-order Fresnel lens with a visibility of 17 miles. The keeper's dwelling was a 2.5-story redbrick duplex. In 1928, the light was upgraded to a third-order Fresnel lens. The lighthouse's daymark was changed to white with an orange-red mid-band. In 1961, the light was fully automated. (Courtesy of the USCG.)

PORT AUSTIN REEF LIGHT, PORT AUSTIN, MICHIGAN. The two-story redbrick duplex along with the square, pyramidal, open framework tower was 80 feet above the lake when built in 1877. A fourth-order Henry-Lepaute lens was used to display a fixed white light, followed by five red flashes. This reef light was only in operation during the shipping season from April through December.

PECHE ISLAND REAR RANGE LIGHTHOUSE, PECHE ISLAND, MICHIGAN, C. 1935. Peche Island is at the confluence of the Detroit River and Lake St. Clair. The Isle aux Peches Range Lights were established in 1898. In 1927, the front range light caught fire, and when the flames reached the acetylene magazine, it exploded. The front tower was blown apart and toppled. The tower consisted of an enclosed conical structural steel plate tower supporting an eight-sided lantern room with a fourth-order fixed lens. The range lights were electrified in 1940. By 1980, the rear range light developed a severe list and was replaced by a modern structure. Michigan National Bank in Port Huron acquired the lighthouse from the company contracted to scrap the light. In 1983, the restored structure was placed on the riverfront in Marine City, Michigan. (Courtesy of the USCG.)

Three

Straits of Mackinac

Old Mackinac Point Lighthouse, Mackinaw City, Michigan. In 1830, Congress felt the Straits of Mackinac should be lit by a lightship and placed one at the Waugoshance Shoal in 1832. However, it was found that the ship was not adequate for the narrow area between Lake Huron and Lake Michigan. In 1888, Congress appropriated funds for a fog signal station to help ships through the narrow area into Mackinaw Harbor. The narrowest point on the straits was near the town of Mackinaw City. But the point would not see a light until the 1890s.

OLD MACKINAC POINT LIGHTHOUSE, MACKINAW CITY, MICHIGAN. In 1892, the tower and keeper's house were built of cream city brick on a limestone foundation. The 40-foot circular tower was 13 feet in diameter. Its octagonal cast-iron lantern housed a fourth-order Fresnel lens with a visibility of 16 miles. The style of the keeper's house was often described as castle-like, with a square tower with a crenelated top. The house was built as a duplex for both the keeper and his assistant. Its tin roof is painted red like the dome of the lantern for use as its daymark. Car ferries crossed the straits, and the lighthouse made it possible for them to run at night. In 1957, when the Mackinac Bridge that crossed over to the Upper Peninsula was opened, the lighthouse was decommissioned. Mackinac State Historical Parks acquired the property in 1960.

McGulpin Point Lighthouse, Mackinaw City, Michigan. In 1868, McGulpin Point was constructed in a Norman Gothic style, with the tower set diagonally into one corner of a 1.5-story keeper's house. Milwaukee cream city brick was used because of its superior strength. A third-and-a-half-order Fresnel lens was placed in the 40-foot-high tower because of the hill on which the lighthouse stands. Although improvements continued for a number of years at the point, after 38 seasons, the light was discontinued in 1906. The light was sold into private ownership soon after. In 2008, Emmet County purchased the light as a museum and gift shop open to the public. (Above, courtesy of the Walter Reuther Library, Wayne State University; below, courtesy of National Archives.)

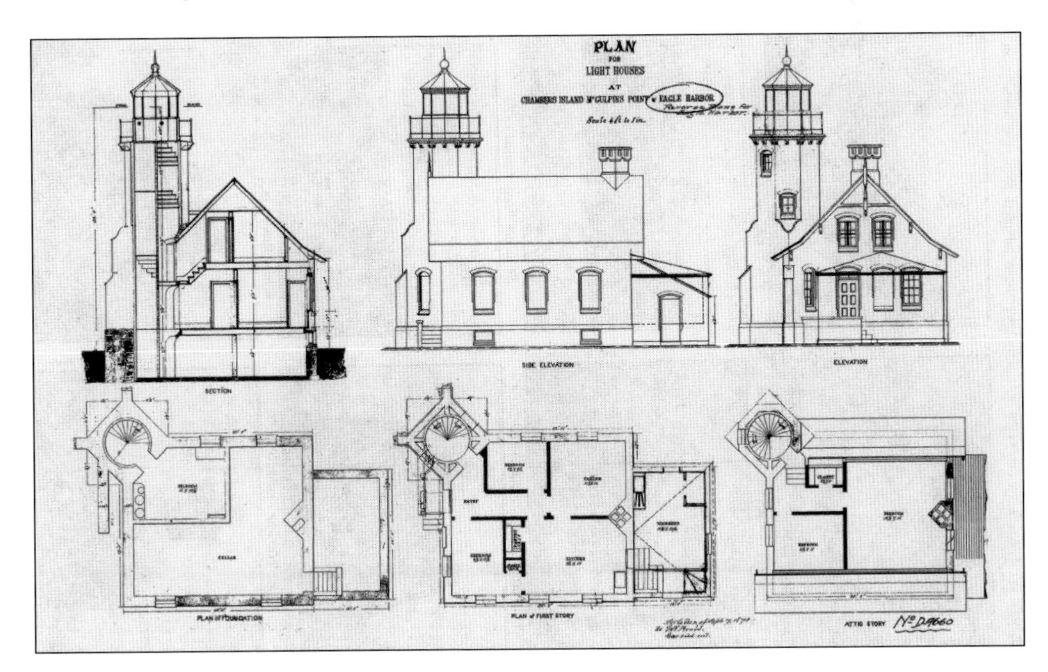

ROUND ISLAND LIGHTHOUSE, MACKINAC ISLAND, MICHIGAN. Before the Round Island light was built, ships took a longer route when passing from Lake Superior to Lake Michigan. Its fourth-order Fresnel lens had a visibility of 14.5 miles. The dwelling was a three-story, redbrick house with a four-story tower, 53 feet high. The first floor held a workroom, the second floor was living quarters for the assistant keepers, and the third floor was for the head keeper during the shipping season. The light was deactivated in 1947. The southwest corner of the light was destroyed during a storm in 1972. Between 1974 and 1976, with help from the Friends of Round Island, the walls and foundation were restored. This quaint lighthouse was made famous in the 1978 film *Somewhere in Time*, starring Christopher Reeve and Jane Seymour.

St. Helena Island Light Station, St. Ignace, Michigan. St. Helena is an uninhabited island in Lake Michigan seven miles west of the Mackinac Bridge and two miles from the Upper Peninsula of Michigan. The 1.5-story brick keeper's house had a covered passageway connecting it to the 71-foot conical tower. With a third-and-a-half-order Fresnel lens, the light marked the hazardous entrance to the Mackinac Straits. In 1922, it was automated. (Courtesy of the USCG.)

Round Island Passage Light, Mackinac Island, Michigan. The Round Island Lighthouse was constructed in 1895 to mark the southern side of the Round Island Channel. In 1947, a need was found for a light on the north side of the channel. A five-story octagonal steel tower 41.5 feet high was built and equipped with a light, fog signal, and radio beacon. This light was one of the last to be built on the Great Lakes, as deactivation had started on many lights.

POE REEF LIGHTHOUSE, CHEBOYGAN, MICHIGAN. The foundation of the Poe Reef Lighthouse is a pier 60 feet square. The superstructure is of steel with a masonry backing. The tower is rectangular, supporting a watch room and a third-order lens and lantern. The first floor housed the mechanical equipment, while the second and third floors held enough space to house the three keepers. Originally painted white, in 1957 the top and bottom third of the light were painted black. It was automated in 1974.

SPECTACLE REEF LIGHTHOUSE, BENTON TOWNSHIP, MICHIGAN. The building of Spectacle Reef light was considered one of the greatest engineering feats of its time in 1874. It took 200 men four years to complete. The tower was 80 feet tall with a visibility of 11 miles. In December 2020, ownership of the Spectacle Reef Lighthouse was transferred to the Spectacle Reef Preservation Society. (Courtesy of the USCG.)

Gray's Reef Lighthouse, Bliss Township, Michigan. This 65-foot tower was built in the Art Deco style and painted bright white in 1936. The base and tower were constructed of steel reinforced concrete, and the lantern room housed a third-and-a-half-order Fresnel lens. In 1965, on a dark, foggy night, the lighthouse was struck by a passing ship without any movement of the light and only minor crib damage. The ship, not needing any assistance, backed up and went on its way to fix its damaged bow. (Courtesy of the USCG.)

Martins Reef Lighthouse, Clark Township, Michigan. In 1927, this light was constructed on a 65-foot-square concrete-filled crib. The lighthouse itself is a 25-foot-square, white, three-story structure made of a steel frame covered in reinforced concrete and iron. A 16-foot-square watch room is at the top of the light with a fourth-order Fresnel lens. The first floor held an engine workroom, and the second floor had offices, a kitchen, and a living area. The third floor contained sleeping quarters. (Courtesy of the USCG.)

White Shoal Lighthouse, Emmet County, Michigan. First lit in 1910, the White Shoal Lighthouse, with its spiraling red stripes, is one of the most distinctive towers in the Great Lakes. The keepers lived inside the nine-story tower. The first floor used to house equipment and fuel, and also provided storage and living quarters. Two bedrooms were on the fourth floor and another bedroom was on the fifth floor along with a sitting room. This was the second light on this shoal, the first being Waugoshance Lighthouse. A 72-foot-square crib was sunk into a gravel base and filled. It is capped with a concrete pier that now sits on a 121-foot, brick-lined steel conical tower with a large clamshell-style lens with a visibility of 28 miles. The tower was originally painted white with a red lantern and dome. In 1954, it was given its distinctive red-and-white barber pole striping for its daymark. This light was automated in 1976. (Courtesy of USCG.)

Four

Lake Superior Lights

Ontonagon Lighthouse, Ontonagon, Michigan. The present schoolhouse-style lighthouse, with a 1.5-story keeper's house and square tower built into the north end, was constructed in 1866 with cream brick. The light tower was 34 feet tall with an iron decagonal lantern that housed a fifth-order Fresnel lens with a visibly of 13 miles. The lighthouse was considered a "welcoming light," meaning it was not there to warn of onshore or offshore hazards, but to aid ships on Lake Superior in finding the harbor. In 1964, the lighthouse was officially decommissioned. In 2003, the Ontonagon County Historical Society received ownership of the lighthouse.

VIDAL SHOAL CHANNEL RANGE LIGHTHOUSE, SAULT STE. MARIE, MICHIGAN. Just before the turn of the 20th century, range lights were placed at the base of the International Train Bridge on the American side of the St. Mary's River to mark the Vidal Shoals and give safe passage into the American Soo Locks that connect Lake Superior to Lake Michigan via the St. Mary's River. The front light was raised about 10 feet to increase its focal plane by having anther iron section placed beneath it. The rear range light was replaced by a new white, octagonal, tapering tower with a slightly higher focal plane. The lights were maintained by the Soo Locks Commission and no longer exist today.

AU SABLE POINT LIGHTHOUSE, GRAND MARIS, LAKE SUPERIOR, MICHIGAN. Because of the 80-mile distance between White Fish Point and Grand Island Harbor, there was a need to construct a new lighthouse. Big Sable Point, also known as Point aux Sables Lighthouse, was built at a site chosen for the towering sand dunes in 1873. A circular 86-foot brick tower was built with a base diameter of 16.5 feet rising to 12 feet, where a watch room housed a third-order Fresnel lens. The tower was painted white for daytime visibility. The 2.5-story keeper's house was attached to the tower by an enclosed passageway. With its distinctive Dutch hip roof construction, it was converted into a double-use residence with the appointment of an assistant keeper. By 1958, the lighthouse was automated and the fog signal removed.

SPLIT ROCK LIGHT STATION, TWO HARBORS, MINNESOTA. This light was built in 1910 by the federal government as a navigational aid in response to a disastrous 1905 storm that sank or damaged 29 ships on western Lake Superior. The keepers lived in three two-story, yellow brick houses built in a row behind the light. The tower was only 38 feet tall, but it stood 168 feet above Lake Superior. The octagonal yellow brick tower sat on a foundation with an ornate concrete ring. The yellow brick continued above a second concrete ring to the gallery and lantern and its black domed top. The third-order Fresnel lens had a visibility of 22 miles. For the first 20 years, the station was only accessible by boat, but by 1924, roads came to the light station and families could live there year-round. The light was retired in 1969.

EAGLE HARBOR LIGHT STATION, EAGLE HARBOR, MICHIGAN. This light sits on the west side of the entrance to Eagle Harbor on Lake Superior. Constructed in the Norman Gothic style in 1870, the light was built with a 1.5-story, seven-room keeper's house with a tower rising from its northeast corner. Built of redbrick, the 44-foot tower is two feet thick at the base with its corners beveled to create an octagonal form. Being the second light built on the spot, the fourth-order Fresnel lens was transferred to the new decagonal lantern room. In 1938, a gale came to area for several days, sweeping waves more than 50 feet high over the lighthouse and burying it in eight inches of ice. The light was automated in 1980.

COPPER HARBOR LIGHTHOUSE, COPPER HARBOR, MICHIGAN. The copper deposits on the Keweenaw Peninsula along Lake Superior's south shore brought many miners to the area. Having to use the lake to export the copper meant that shipping in the area increased. In 1868, a new lighthouse was built to replace the old one because of disrepair when the first one was constructed in 1849. The new light was built in the schoolhouse style and was placed 77 feet east of the original. Stone from the old light was used in the foundation of the new tower and house. The square 42-foot tower had a decagonal iron lantern with a fourth-order Fresnel lens and a visibility of 15 miles. In 1957, the US Coast Guard sold the light to the State of Michigan.

Outer Island Lighthouse, Apostle Islands, Bayfield, Wisconsin. Standing on a high bluff at the most remote point of the Apostle Island chain, the Outer Island Lighthouse was built in 1874 to help guide ships past the archipelago to the ports of Duluth and Superior. Built in the Italianate architectural style, its 78-foot brick walls rise to support a circular iron gallery with 16 ornate corbels and a lantern room, which held a third-order Fresnel lens and had a visibility of 20 miles. The keeper's house was a 2.5-story redbrick home with a hipped roof, and an enclosed wooden passageway provided entry to the tower. While the house retained its redbrick color, the tower was stuccoed over and whitewashed to make its daymark highly visible. Because of the remoteness of the light, keepers were rotated frequently. The light was automated in 1961.

BIG BAY POINT LIGHTHOUSE, BIG BAY, MICHIGAN. This lighthouse was built in 1868 on a high cliff at the east side of Big Bay on the southern shore of Lake Superior. The keeper's house was an 18-room duplex with a square 60-foot tower rising up the middle of the north side of the dwelling. Both duplex interiors were almost identical: six rooms on the first floor consisting of a kitchen, parlor, and dining room and three bedrooms on the second floor, but only the keeper had direct access to the office. The keeper's privy had a window, but the assistant's did not! The fifth level of the five-story tower housed a third-order Fresnel lens with a visibility of 16 miles. The light was electrified in 1940. In 1961, the US Coast Guard sold the lighthouse into private hands. (Both, courtesy of Nick Korstad and the Big Bay Point Lighthouse.)

Crisp Point Lighthouse, Newberry, Michigan. This station operated on a desolate section of the Lake Superior shore in 1876 as the Crisp Point Lifesaving Station. In 1902, Congress appropriated $18,000 for a lighthouse and 15 acres of land. The site included a light tower, two cottages for station families, and utility buildings. Usually onsite were just a keeper, his two assistants and their families, and the lifesaving crew of nine. The tower is a 58-foot, double-brick conical tower with an octagonal cast-iron lantern for a fourth-order Fresnel lens and black wrought iron railing surrounding the gallery. In 1930, the light became automated. In 1997, the Coast Guard transferred the light to Luce County. (Both, courtesy of the Crisp Point Historical Society.)

Whitefish Point Light Station, Paradise, Michigan. Whitefish Point is known as the "graveyard of Superior" because of the wrecks lost off the point, including the *Edmund Fitzgerald* freighter on November 10, 1975. A larger, taller lighthouse and keeper's house were built in 1857. A fourth-order Fresnel lens, with a visibility of 13 miles, was installed in the lantern of the 78-foot-tall tower with four levels. The second floor of the keeper's house attaches to the tower through a passage, with a spiral staircase inside the shaft of the tower that gives access to the decagonal lantern room. This new tower was designed as an iron-pile tower to withstand high winds from the lake. The cylinder had four tubular iron legs bolted to a foundation. The light station was fully automated in 1971. The image below is from around 1890. (Above, courtesy of the Michigan State Archives.)

PORTAGE LAKE SHIP CANAL LIGHTHOUSE, HOUGHTON, MICHIGAN. Portage Lake was 17 miles long and had a three-mile, shallow, twisting river that flowed into Keweenaw Bay. It was found that this waterway was an excellent refuge when Lake Superior became violent and easier than going around the Keweenaw Peninsula that protrudes over halfway across the lake. In 1874, a large two-story, two-keeper brick house was built with an attached 43-foot-high square brick tower. In the lantern room was a three-and-a-half-order Fresnel lens. Many additions and changes occurred at the Portage Lake Ship Canal Lighthouse over the years, but it became fully automated during the 1970s, and many of the building were torn down or sold to private owners.

SAND ISLAND LIGHTHOUSE, BAYFIELD, WISCONSIN, C. 1913. The Sand Island Lighthouse, one of the many Apostle Island lights, is on the northern tip of Sand Island. In 1881, a 44-foot tower was built into the northwest corner of the living quarters. It had a square base that turned into an octagonal top that was circular inside. It housed a fourth-order Fresnel lens with a visibility of 20 miles. The keeper's house, built with yellow Milwaukee brick, was a 1.5-story building with living quarters on the main floor and two bedrooms on the upper floor. The gables on the keeper's house had gingerbread ornaments and ornamental stonework above the windows. The light was transferred to a new 48-foot steel skeletal tower erected in 1933.

Mendota (Bete Grise) Lighthouse, Bete Grise, Delaware, Michigan. Originally, in 1867, this was a pier light with a 1.5-story keeper's house on the shore nearby. By 1870, it was felt that the pier light was ineffectual, and it was decommissioned. A new lighthouse was built in 1895 with a 44-foot tower and a fourth-order lens; it extended from the middle of the east side of the 1.5-story keeper's house. The light was decommissioned in 1956.

Sand Point Lighthouse, Baraga, Michigan, c. 1922. A lighthouse was built at L'Anse Bay in 1877. Plans called for a rectangular, 1.5-story keeper's house with an 8.5-foot square tower facing the lake. Built with redbrick, the tower accessed the lantern room and both floors of the five-room dwelling. The light was sold into private ownership in 1933.

Menagerie Island Lighthouse, Isle Royal, Houghton Township, Michigan. In 1875, a tower and keeper's house were built of red Jacobsville sandstone quarried from the Keweenaw Peninsula. The 55-foot octagonal tower had a decagonal lantern room with a fourth-order Fresnel lens made in Paris with a visibility of 15 miles. The 1.5-story keeper's house had a hipped roof covered in cedar shake shingles and iron shutters to protect the windows from extreme weather. The light was automated in 1913. (Courtesy of Jacob W. Frank.)

Passage Island Lighthouse, Isle Royal, Houghton Township, Michigan. The Passage Island Light is 3.25 miles northeast of Isle Royal in Lake Superior. Both the tower and the 1.5-story keeper's house were made of coarse fieldstone left in its natural finish. The house had living quarters and two bedrooms upstairs with access to the tower from each floor. Using a fourth-order Fresnel lens, it had a visibility of 16 miles. The 37-foot tower was set diagonally into the corner of the house.

Rock Harbor Lighthouse, Isle Royal, Houghton Township, Michigan. This lighthouse was a combined 1.5-story keeper's house and 50-foot tower. The house was a 29-foot square on a stone foundation of coursed rubble stone walls. It had two smaller brick chimneys. Included in the house were an office, living quarters with kitchen, and a walk-through passage into the tower from the first floor. The conical tower was built of brick and stone and housed a fourth-order Fresnel lens with a visibility of 14 miles. It was built in 1855 on the mainland of Isle Royal at the south end of the rock-covered Middle Islands Passage. The light was closed in 1859. It was relit in 1874 but was closed once again by 1879.

MICHIGAN ISLAND LIGHTHOUSE, APOSTLE ISLANDS, LA POINTE, WISCONSIN. Located in the western Lake Superior Apostle Islands, the Michigan Island Lighthouse was constructed in 1857; however, it was not activated until 1869. The first light, seen here, was in service until 1929, when construction began on a new 118-foot skeletal tower with a three-and-a-half-order Fresnel lens with a visibility of 22 miles. By 1943, the lamp became fully automated.

DEVIL'S ISLAND LIGHTHOUSE, APOSTLE ISLAND, LA POINTE, WISCONSIN. A two-story Queen Anne–style keeper's house was built with a temporary wood tower at 87 feet above the lake level. It housed a fourth-order Fresnel lens with a visibility of 13 miles. In 1897, work began on a permanent 71-foot cast-iron cylindrical tower; it took three years to get a new third-order lens. The light was automated in 1978.

Point Iroquois Light Station, Brimley, Michigan. The new light built in 1879 was a 65-foot-tall conical redbrick tower attached to a 1.5-story redbrick keeper's house. The house and tower were painted white for better visibility. With its polygonal cast-iron lantern, it housed a fourth-order Fresnel lens, giving it visibility for 16 miles out into the lake. The light was automated in 1962.

Jacobsville (Portage River) Lighthouse, Lake Linden, Michigan. The second lighthouse built on the 30-foot bluff, in 1870, was a 1.5-story brick keeper's house with a covered passageway that led to the 45-foot cylindrical stone tower. The exterior of the house and tower were whitewashed to make the daymark more visible. The lantern room housed a fifth-order Fresnel lens with a visibility of 15 miles. The light was discontinued in 1919. In 1958, the Jacobsville light was sold into private ownership.

DULUTH HARBOR SOUTH BREAKWATER OUTER LIGHTHOUSE, DULUTH, MINNESOTA. When harbor improvements were made and the pier lengthened, a new permanent light was built in 1902, making the 1872 light, seven-room keeper's house, and elevated walkway obsolete. The fog signal and lighthouse were built with white brick and a red metal roof. Inside, the circular lantern room housed a fourth-order Fresnel lens, giving the lamp a visibility of 12 miles.

GRAND MARAIS LIGHTHOUSE, GRAND MARAIS, MINNESOTA. In 1885, the government approved funds for a lighthouse at Grand Marais. Breakwater piers were erected at the mouth of the bay. The tower's lantern came from surplus at the Detroit depot, and the light housed a fifth-order Fresnel lens made by the Louis Sautter Company of Paris. The tower was a 32-foot, square, wooden, pyramidal structure completely enclosed, with an octagonal lantern room. The light was automated in 1932.

MARQUETTE HARBOR LIGHTHOUSE, MARQUETTE, MICHIGAN. This new light built in 1866 had a 1.5-story keeper's dwelling with a center-front light tower in the schoolhouse style. The tower was 38 feet high and 78 feet above the water. With a white decagonal lantern and a fourth-order Fresnel lens, it had a visibility of 19 miles. The light was extinguished in 1929.

GRAND MARAIS INNER HARBOR LIGHT, GRAND MARAIS, MICHIGAN. A need was found for a safe harbor between Whitefish Bay and Grand Island on Lake Superior. A skeleton iron tower and elevated walk, along with a fog signal, were bolted to the pier. Painted white, the tower stood 34 feet tall, and its octagonal iron lantern housed a sixth-order Fresnel lens. Because no keeper's quarters were built, the first lighthouse personnel lived in a temporary shanty.

Grand Island East Channel Lighthouse, Munising, Michigan. This lighthouse was built on a low sandy area on the southwest side of Grand Island in 1867. To minimize the costs related to building this lighthouse, it was constructed of timber and wood siding instead of stronger materials, but it was placed on a stone foundation. The 1.5-story keeper's house had a square 45-foot tower attached to the south end of the building. The house and tower were painted white for an easily seen daymark. A fourth-order Fresnel lens with a visibility of 13.5 miles was housed in its lantern room. In 1908, the light was extinguished after range lights became active.

Five

Lake Erie Lights

Old Barcelona Lighthouse, Westfield, New York, 1905. On a bluff overlooking Portland Harbor in the town of Westfield, one of the earliest lighthouses on the Great Lakes was built in 1829. With the opening of the Erie Canal, Portland Harbor, now known as Barcelona, was designated an official port of entry with the increase in shipping to the area. Congress appropriated $5,000 for the building of the Old Barcelona Lighthouse.

OLD BARCELONA LIGHTHOUSE, WESTFIELD, NEW YORK. The 40-foot conical tower has a base diameter of 22 feet. The rough stone walls are 3.5 feet thick near the base and taper up to 10.5 feet diameter. The light was originally lit by 11 lamps and 11 reflectors and fueled by oil. When natural gas was found in the area, it was lit by gas until that vein ran out and the keepers went back to oil. The keeper's house was 34 feet by 20 feet and built with rough-cut stone. It had a center-placed chimney to heat both rooms of the house. It was fitted with a fourth-order Fresnel lens in 1857, but by 1859, the light was discontinued due to less use of the harbor after the railroad came through the area. It has been in private hands for many years.

MARBLEHEAD LIGHTHOUSE, ROCKY POINT, OHIO. The limestone tower was built in 1870 from stone quarried from Marblehead, Ohio. The base was 26 feet in diameter with walls five feet thick. The top measured 12 feet in diameter with walls two feet thick in its 50-foot-high tower. In 1858, with whale oil becoming expensive, a Fresnel lens was added. By 1897, a 15-foot extension was added to raise the light along with a fourth-order Fresnel lens. In 1880, a new wood frame keeper's house was built to replace the original home constructed in 1821. It still stands today. Rather than build a new structure in 1897, the top eight feet of the limestone tower were moved and a cylindrical brick extension, which housed a watch room, was added to the top. The light was automated in 1958.

ASHTABULA HARBOR LIGHTHOUSE, ASHTABULA, OHIO. Located near the northern end of the west breakwater in Ashtabula Harbor, this light was constructed as the harbor developed. The first light was built in 1836 on the east pier sandlot. In 1876, a new taller light was built on the west pierhead, and in 1896, a fourth-order Fresnel lens was added. In 1905, a large two-story square building was erected at the end of a new breakwater, with a round tower and lantern room on top of the structure. The fourth-order lens was used once again. By 1973, the light was automated. The keeper's house was sold into private ownership. In 1984, the Ashtabula Historical Society purchased the light.

Presque Isle Lighthouse, Erie, Pennsylvania. A peninsula, six miles long, protrudes into the waters of Lake Erie forming a large natural harbor. In 1870, plans were underway for the Presque Isle light to replace the Erie Land light. The tower is 70 feet high to the ventilator ball, with five courses of brick in order to withstand the fierce storms and winds coming off the lake. The original light had a polygonal lantern with a fourth-order Fresnel lens and, with the use of whale oil, had a visibility of 15 miles. The keeper's quarters was a two-story brick structure with 10 rooms. Today, the tower is painted white and has a black lantern, dome, and ventilator ball. The lighthouse was transferred in 2014 into the hands of a nonprofit organization to open as a museum.

West Sister Island Lighthouse, Jerusalem Township, Ohio. By 1848, a lighthouse was built on the western point of West Sister Island to mark the southern passage through Lake Erie's Bass Islands. A 40-foot conical-shaped tower was constructed of stone, and a keeper's house measuring 20 by 30 feet was built near the tower. Improvements were needed by 1868 as the lighthouse was deteriorating. The keeper's quarters got a second story by 1902. The light was automated in 1937 and the keeper's quarters abandoned. The island was used for artillery practice during World War II. The light is still active in aiding navigation. (Below, courtesy of the National Archives.)

FAIRPORT HARBOR LIGHTHOUSE, FAIRPORT HARBOR, OHIO. Lake Erie is the shallowest of the Great Lakes, and storms can overtake ships very quickly on its smooth surface. The first light here was constructed in 1825; unfortunately, within a few years, it began to show signs of wear because of foundation issues. In 1870, a 69-foot-high conical tower of grey-brown Berea sandstone was built. The decagonal lantern with a third-order Fresnel lens gave a 17.5-mile visibility. The two-story keeper's house was built of redbrick and finished in 1871. The light was obsolete by 1925. The station was used as part of the underground railway before the Civil War and helped many escaping slaves reach safety in Canada. The image at right is from around 1906.

LIGHT HOUSE, PUT-IN-BAY, OHIO

SOUTH BASS ISLAND LIGHTHOUSE, PUT-IN-BAY, OHIO. With the South Passage now acting as the primary navigational route not just for commercial shipping but also passenger boats, the increased traffic began causing concerns for safety. Not designed in typical lighthouse fashion, in 1896, construction began on the South Bass Island Lighthouse. It consisted of a large, 2.5-story, redbrick dwelling with an attached 12-foot tower. Its Queen Anne style with ornately spindled verandas on the front and back gave it a very quaint look. When finished, the tower stood 45 feet high and housed a fourth-order Fresnel lens in the white decagonal lantern room. In 1962, the light was automated. By 1983, the National Oceanic and Atmospheric Administration installed a meteorological station at the site. While no longer open to the public, the light can still be seen from the water.

DUNKIRK (POINT GRATIOT) LIGHTHOUSE, DUNKIRK, NEW YORK. Sitting on a 20-foot bluff, the large, square tower and keeper's house are the second lighthouse to serve the Point Gratiot area. In 1857, it was repurposed with a third-order Fresnel lens with a 17-mile visibility. But because of deterioration, in 1875, a new limestone tower was built and the old lens was transferred to the new tower. The keeper's house, constructed in High Victorian Gothic style, was built with redbrick. There was delicate, ornamental cross bracing under the eaves and a dormer rising out of the brick walls. The doors and trim are painted white to stand out against the redbrick. A covered passage connects the tower to the residence. The light was electrified in 1923.

Belle Isle Light Station, Detroit, Michigan. Belle Isle is located where the Detroit River meets the St. Clair River, and in 1882, the government built a brick lighthouse in the Victorian style with gingerbread trim and elaborate brickwork. A 5.5-foot tower was attached. The fourth-order Fresnel lens was visible for 13 miles. The date the light was extinguished is not known, but by 1941, the lighthouse was demolished.

Mama Juda Lighthouse, Detroit, Michigan. On the Detroit River lies a marshy, low-lying, three-acre island named after a Native American woman called Mama Juda. When the fish were running, this area was where she set up a fishing camp each season. Over the years, three lighthouses were built on the island, including the third one pictured here with a 1.5-story keeper's house with a dormer in the roof and a cylindrical masonry tower extending two stories above the house with a polygonal iron lantern room. By 1920, it was automated.

ERIE LAND LIGHTHOUSE, ERIE, PENNSYLVANIA. In 1867, on a high bluff overlooking Erie Bay, a 49-foot circular, unpainted tower was built with a decagonal lantern topped with a white fluted dome. The lantern housed a third-order Fresnel lens with a visibility of 17 miles. A two-story Saltbox-style keeper's house was built separately from the light tower. By 1901, with the new Presque Isle light, the Erie light was extinguished. The town took over the care and upkeep of the light in 1934.

Vermilion Pier Light, Vermilion, Ohio. The third light to be built in Vermilion Harbor in 1877 was a 34-foot octagonal tapering tower placed on a concrete foundation at the end of a wooden pier. A 400-foot catwalk was also added. The bottom of the tower was painted reddish-brown, and the upper part painted white with a black lantern room. Its fifth-order Fresnel lens had a visibility of nine miles. It was automated in 1919.

Port Clinton Lighthouse, Port Clinton, Ohio. The first lighthouse, built in 1833, was a round, pyramidal tower made of split stone, standing 40 feet tall with lamps and reflectors to project a beam of light 10 miles. A single-story, 20-by-34-foot stone keeper's house was built near the tower. The lighthouse was discontinued in 1859, with a reactivation in 1864. In 1870, the lantern room was removed and the light deactivated for good.

LORAIN WEST BREAKWATER LIGHTHOUSE, LORAIN, OHIO, C. 1919. Due to harbor growth in the late 1800s, the Lorain West Breakwater Lighthouse was built in 1917. On a concrete foundation, a building 3.5-stories tall was built with the tower extending one more story from the roof with a circular lantern room with a fourth-order Fresnel lens. In 1965, the light was slated for demolition, but in 1977 the Lorain Historical Society took over the deed.

DETROIT RIVER LIGHT STATION, BERLIN CHARTER TOWNSHIP, MICHIGAN. In 1884, a timber crib was towed to a location with a depth of 22 feet and filled with concrete. A cut granite stone block pier was mounted on it. A 49-foot, spark-plug type cast-iron plate tower was placed on the pier with a decagonal-shaped lantern room. It housed a fourth-order Fresnel lens with a visibility of 25 miles. It was painted white on the bottom and black on top. The light was automated in 1979.

BUFFALO OLD MAIN LIGHTHOUSE, BUFFALO, NEW YORK. In 1833, a new light with a 44-foot octagonal tapering tower was built of buff-colored Queenston limestone. In 1857, the original lantern was removed and additional stories were added to accommodate a fog bell and a fourth-order Fresnel lens. The new decagonal lantern room with a round iron pedestal room made the new tower 68 feet from the base to the top of the ventilator ball. It was painted white in 1900 for a brighter daymark. In 1958, the Coast Guard wanted to demolish it when making harbor improvements; however, in 1961, it transferred ownership of the light to the Buffalo and Erie Historical Society. This is the oldest lighthouse tower in Buffalo and also the oldest in its original location.

Six

Lake Ontario Lights

Selkirk Lighthouse, Pulaski, New York, c. 1910. The Selkirk Lighthouse, originally called the Salmon Point River Light Station, stands as an early monument to construction and function in its unique structure and appearance. With its "birdcage" lantern room—a hexagonal dome of glass and iron—its optic was a 14-inch parabolic reflector with eight mineral oil lamps that could be seen for 14 miles. During Prohibition, the light became very popular with local smugglers.

SELKIRK LIGHTHOUSE, PULASKI, NEW YORK. When Congress agreed to $3,000 in March 1837 for a lighthouse, land was purchased from Sylvester and Daniel Brown as a site for the building. Plans called to construct a two-story lighthouse with an octagonal tower that would extend 16 feet above the building. Local stonemason Jabez Meacham used stone from a local quarry, and blacksmith John Box created the wrought iron railing and surround for the birdcage lantern room. Shortly after the lighthouse was completed, a canal was proposed for connecting the Salmon River to the Hudson River and the Erie Canal, but when the canal proposal fell through, the importance of the harbor diminished, and the Salmon River Lighthouse was deactivated in 1859. The property has remained in private hands through the years.

THIRTY MILE POINT LIGHTHOUSE, BARKER, NEW YORK. This lighthouse got its name because it is 30 miles east of the Niagara River on Lake Ontario. It was built as a coastal light to warn ships of approaching shoals and to guide them along this portion of Lake Ontario. In 1876, a two-story, seven-room keeper's quarters and the attached 70-foot-tall square tower were built in the Victorian Gothic style using natural-faced limestone blocks from the Dewey and Phelps limestone quarry near Chaumont Bay. The tower's six-panel, third-order Fresnel lens was built in France by L. Sautter and Company. Over the years, shoreline erosion became a great concern, and a series of jetties were constructed. It was 1921 before a fog signal was added to the station. The light was decommissioned in 1958.

Horse Island Lighthouse, Sackets Harbor, New York. Horse Island is a 28-acre island about a mile west of the harbor and attached to the mainland by a causeway. While the first light was built in 1831, by 1870 a replacement light was needed. A square tower attached to the front of the 1.5-story keeper's quarters was built of redbrick. It was four stories tall with a circular lantern that housed a fifth-order Fresnel lens. At an unknown date, an additional 10 feet were added to the tower and additions were made to the keeper's quarters. The tower and quarters were painted white and the lantern room black. In 1957, the light was deactivated, and by 1963, the lantern room was painted red. The island and lighthouse are now under private ownership. (Above, courtesy of USCG.)

Tibbetts Point Lighthouse, Cape Vincent, New York. A lighthouse was built at Tibbetts Point to make navigating the entrance into the St. Lawrence River easier. The first light was built in 1827, but there were complaints of its inefficiency. In 1854, a 61-foot cylindrical tower finished in white stucco was built. It used a fourth-order Fresnel lens. The station included the tower with an attached small room, a steam-powered fog signal building, and an iron oil house. By 1880, a two-story brick keeper's house replaced the old lodgings. The US Coast Guard took responsibility in 1939. The light was automated in the 1970s, and Coast Guard personnel remained on post until 1981. The Town of Cape Vincent acquired the light station in 1991.

Sodus Point Lighthouse, Sodus Point, New York. The second lighthouse to be built at Sodus Point was completed in 1871 with a 45-foot, limestone square tower and an attached 2.5-story keeper's house constructed with split stone. The pyramidal-shaped tower housed a fourth-order Fresnel lens set on a concrete pier. The stone used for the first light was reused to build a jetty and help stop erosion. Both the lighthouse and the pier light worked simultaneously from early 1834 until 1901, when use of the main station light was discontinued on the bluff. The Town of Sodus Point was handed responsibility for the lighthouse and its outer buildings from the Coast Guard in 1984; it is now maintained by the Sodus Point Historical Society. The image below is from before 1906.

OGDENSBURG HARBOR LIGHTHOUSE, OGDENSBURG, NEW YORK. Where the Oswegatchie and the St. Lawrence Rivers meet, a lighthouse was needed to warn mariners to keep to the deeper water near the Canadian shore. The light was built on a low, rocky point 200 feet above the harbor to mark the area. In 1870, the 40-foot, white limestone square tower housed a fourth-order Fresnel lens. A 1.5-story keeper's quarters, built of square-cut, rough-faced limestone obtained from the Kingston quarries, had a mixed style of an Italianate tower and a Queen Anne–influenced house. In 1892, a new and larger kitchen and porch were added to the rear of the house. The tower was increased to 65 feet in 1900 with additional limestone brickwork. The light was discontinued in 1961 and sold to private owners.

ROCK ISLAND LIGHTHOUSE, FISHER'S LANDING, NEW YORK. Four and a half miles from Clayton, New York, in the St. Lawrence River stands a small island of rock. In 1848, a lighthouse was needed to create a safe passage through the head of the narrows for the Thousand Islands on the south side. By 1882, a lighthouse was built with a 40-foot tower and a two-story, Shingle-style keeper's house. A carpenter's house and machinery building were also constructed. Part of the tower on the bottom was concrete and limestone while the upper portion was made of iron. The tower was moved to the end of a 10-foot-long pier on the north side of the island. The lantern room housed a sixth-order Fresnel lens with a visibility of 12 miles. The lighthouse was deactivated in 1958.

FORT NIAGARA LIGHTHOUSE, YOUNGSTOWN, NEW YORK. The third lighthouse to be built on the American side of the Niagara River was started in 1871 on the banks of the river just south of Fort Niagara. The octagonal limestone tower started at a height of 45 feet, but its focal plane was raised 11 feet in 1900 when a brick watch room was added between the top of the stone tower and the lantern room. The decagonal lantern held a fourth-order Fresnel lens that had been transferred from the old light; it still had a visibility of 23 miles. The US Coast Guard decommissioned the light in 1993. Currently, it is used as a museum by the Old Fort Niagara Association.

CHARLOTTE-GENESEE LIGHTHOUSE, ROCHESTER, NEW YORK. The need for a lighthouse had long been established when in 1822 an octagonal limestone tower 40 feet in height was built. Its lantern room was eight-sided and contained 144 panes of glass. In 1853, the lamps were replaced with a fourth-order Fresnel lens. In 1862, the keeper's quarters were replaced with a 2.5-story, eight-room brick house. The keeper's quarters were connected to the tower by a brick passageway. In 1881, the lighthouse that sat on the bluff was deactivated. When the US Coast Guard vacated the site in 1981, the Charlotte-Genesee Lighthouse Historical Society of Monroe County was formed to restore the light and create a museum. (Below, courtesy of the Library of Congress.)

Braddock Point Lighthouse, Hilton, New York. The 110-foot brick tower was attached to the 2.5-story redbrick keeper's house, built in 1896 in the Victorian style. The tower had a high arched dome with ribbing to join the panels and a ventilator ball and lightning rod. A three-and-a-half-order Fresnel lens gave an 18-mile visibility out on the lake. The light remained in operation until 1954, when it was decommissioned. Soon after, two thirds of the tower were torn down because of deterioration. The destruction stopped when the light was sold into private ownership. The tower was later rebuilt to a height of 65 feet, and the Coast Guard relit it, giving it a visibility of 15 miles. (Both, courtesy of the National Archives.)

STONY POINT LIGHTHOUSE, HENDERSON HARBOR, NEW YORK. The house built at Stony Point in 1869 was a large 1.5-story keeper's house. Built with cut limestone blocks, it is painted white and trimmed in black. The 73-foot, white square tower faces the lake side of the house. The original light was a fourth-order Fresnel lens. The light was deactivated in 1945 and sold into private ownership. (Courtesy of the USCG.)

GALLO ISLAND LIGHTHOUSE, HOUNSFIELD, NEW YORK. This island marks the outer edge of a group of islands and shoals that guard the entrance to the St. Lawrence River. The second light, shown here, was erected in 1867. The stone conical-shaped tower is 55 feet high and has a 1.5-story attached keeper's house. Built of gray limestone quarried from the island, the light was automated in 1963. Today, Gallo Island is privately owned. (Courtesy of the USCG.)

OSWEGO WEST PIERHEAD LIGHT, OSWEGO, NEW YORK. In 1836, a light was built at the west end of a new pier to mark the harbor entrance. The light was a tapering gray stone octagonal structure with an attached oil and mechanical room. It had 13 lamps and reflectors to display a white fixed light. By 1868, the tower was raised 25 feet, and a third-order Fresnel lens was added to give a visibility of 15 miles. The light was dismantled in 1929.

OSWEGO BREAKWATER LIGHTHOUSE, OSWEGO, NEW YORK. In 1932, a new breakwater light was constructed at the end of the western pier. The light had a concrete foundation that extended 10 feet out of the water to help deflect waves. The small, square, white, two-story keeper's house had a red pyramidal roof. The square tower extended up past the house for two stories, and its white polygonal lantern room housed a fourth-order Fresnel lens.

SUNKEN ROCK LIGHTHOUSE, ALEXANDRIA BAY, NEW YORK. During the summer of 1847, an octagonal brick tower, 31 feet high, was built to mark the entrance to the narrow passage where the shipping channel runs between Wellesley Island and the mainland. The island was so tiny that no keeper's quarters were built there. Sunken Rock Lighthouse received a sixth-order lens in 1855.

CROSS-OVER ISLAND LIGHTHOUSE, HAMMOND, NEW YORK. On a small island among the Thousand Islands in the St. Lawrence River sits a small, white lighthouse. The island got its name because it marked the point where ships crossed between American waters and the Canadian Channel. In 1882, a new tower was built of iron and painted white with a red lantern room housing a sixth-order Fresnel lens. Decommissioned in 1941, today it is privately owned.

SODUS OUTER LIGHTHOUSE, SODUS POINT, NEW YORK. In 1901, the fourth-order Fresnel lens used in the Sodus Bay Lighthouse was removed and transferred to the outer pier tower, which had been elevated 15 feet using concrete piers to give it a focal plane of 45 feet. In 1938, the wood tower was replaced with the current cast-iron structure, and the light was converted to electric.

CHARLOTTE-GENESEE WEST PIERHEAD LIGHT, ROCHESTER, NEW YORK. A pair of 2,600-foot-long piers were built at the mouth of the river in 1829. Badly damaged by storms, a second light was placed there in 1854 using a sixth-order Fresnel lens. In 1884, a new 28-foot, white, square, tapering wooden tower with a decagonal lantern room was built to replace the previous light, using a fourth-order Fresnel lens.

FAIR HAVEN LIGHTHOUSE, FAIR HAVEN, NEW YORK. In 1872, Congress decided to build a frame beacon, which was shipped from Oswego and erected on the west pier. The light had a fourth-order Fresnel lens showing a fixed white light. In 1873, an elevated walkway was built from the beach to the beacon. By 1880, the walkway needed total rebuilding. By 1882, the beacon was moved out 240 feet and the walkway extended. Though many further changes occurred over the years, by 1949, the Fair Haven light was electrified and its candlepower increased to 200.

Seven

Lifesaving Stations

Point Betsie Lifesaving Station, Lake Michigan, Michigan, c. 1913. A lifesaving station was completed just south of Point Betsie in 1876 to help mariners who found themselves in trouble in the Manitous Passage. Pictured here demonstrating the need for lifesaving stations, a lifesaving crew is helping a drowning victim. Point Betsie sits in the background.

South Haven Lifesaving Station, Lake Michigan, Michigan. The Coast Guard station in South Haven was built in 1872, with both the land and the building acquired in the same year. The property was located in South Haven, Van Buren County, Michigan. The station moved to the south side of the harbor entrance in 1905. The lifesaving station was occupied until 1972 and deactivated in 1973.

Cleveland Lifesaving Station, Lake Erie, Ohio. In 1875, Cleveland became part of District 9 of the US Life-Saving Service, operating as a lifeboat service from November through April, a very active season. A group of eight crewmen and a keeper worked at weekly drills while housed at the life station. The crewmen understood the severity of their rescue missions and lived by the motto "We've got to go out, but we don't have to come back," a strong testament to their dedication.

MACATAWA LIFESAVING STATION, LAKE MICHIGAN, MICHIGAN. Coast Guard Station No. 217 was in Holland, Michigan, on the south side of the entrance to Lake Macatawa, one-eighth of a mile east of the south pier rear range light. Land for the lifeboat station was acquired in both 1875 and 1884.

CHARLEVOIX LIFESAVING STATION, LAKE MICHIGAN, MICHIGAN. This station was first built in 1898 on the south breakwall of the Pine River Channel leading into Lake Michigan. It was officially commissioned as a US Lifesaving Station in 1900. During the 1960s, the station was relocated to its present location along the Pine River Channel's Lake Charlevoix end.

ST. JOSEPH LIFESAVING STATION, LAKE MICHIGAN, MICHIGAN, PRE-1907. In 1855, the federal government began supplying equipment for use in maritime rescues. Many of the lifesaving crew were paid $10 a month but were laid off in the winter. This Coast Guard station was originally established in 1874. The lifesaving building was constructed north of the lighthouse in 1898.

FRANKFORT LIFESAVING STATION, LAKE MICHIGAN, MICHIGAN, PRE-1907. The long history between the Coast Guard and Frankfort began in 1887 when the US Life-Saving Service established a station on the Elberta side of the harbor. That station is still standing about 1.5 miles from where the current station sits today, full restored. In 1934, a new station was built on the Frankfort side of the harbor.

KENOSHA LIFESAVING STATION, LAKE MICHIGAN, WISCONSIN. The first station in Kenosha was built in 1879. The station responded to 2,307 calls for assistance from 1879 to 1935. In 1907, the Kenosha station received the first motor-driven lifesaving boat on Lake Michigan. A new station was constructed in 1934 to replace the original buildings from 1879.

CHICAGO LIFESAVING STATION, LAKE MICHIGAN, ILLINOIS. Built in 1875, the Chicago Lifesaving Station had a lifeboat detachment as early as 1878. The worst marine disaster within the scope of operations of this station was the capsizing of the steamer *Eastland* on July 24, 1915, with 2,400 passengers on board. A total of 280 people were rescued by the Chicago crew, and 400 bodies were recovered. It was estimated that this station was involved in saving at least 6,000 lives through 1935.

MILWAUKEE LIFESAVING STATION, LAKE MICHIGAN, WISCONSIN. Built in 1878, Life Saving Station No. 10 was created for the volunteers of the US Life-Saving Service. The station was at the mouth of the Milwaukee River and was considered the fourth-largest station in the district. The new Shingle-style station lasted nearly 30 years. By 1915, it was abandoned due to unsanitary water conditions.

STURGEON BAY SHIP CANAL LIFESAVING STATION, LAKE MICHIGAN, WISCONSIN. This station was built in 1886 after the completion of the privately owned Sturgeon Bay & Lake Michigan Ship Canal in 1880. Land was transferred to the federal government in 1884 for both a light and a lifesaving station. Later, due to shifting of the refining wall on the north side of the canal, the project required the station to be jacked up and moved back 50 feet.

LUDINGTON LIFESAVING STATION, LAKE MICHIGAN, MICHIGAN. By 1878, a lifeboat station was authorized for Ludington. At this time, the boats were manned by volunteers who would manage a single lifeboat, rowing it out to aid mariners in distress. For the next two decades, despite the handicaps, these courageous volunteers saved many lives. It was not until 1934 that a lifesaving station was built, with wooden lifeboats mounted on rails inside the station. As technology progressed and lifeboats became larger, the boats were kept near the docks.

RACINE LIFESAVING STATION, LAKE MICHIGAN, WISCONSIN. A lifesaving station was added to the harbor in 1903; it was a two-story, square, pyramidal-roofed lookout tower. Included with the station was a framed boathouse. A team from the US Life-Saving Service lived at the station. Search and rescue operations were conducted along the Milwaukee and Kenosha coastline and 40 miles out into Lake Michigan.

LORAIN LIFESAVING STATION, LAKE ERIE, OHIO. A lot on the east bank of the Black River was donated by the city. Although most of it was swampland, a lifesaving station opened in Lorain in 1910 with an eight-man crew. Described as one of the finest stations on the Great Lakes, it included a new power lifeboat, which had a 25-horsepower engine and three sails, and would hold 10 oarsmen.

HARBOR BEACH LIFESAVING STATION, LAKE HURON, MICHIGAN. Over the years, four stations were built at Harbor Beach: 1881, 1910, 1935, and 1987. Each station used improvements to make the lifesaving process quicker and safer for the crews. From 1876 to 1878, the growing network of lifesaving stations was finally organized as a separate agency of the Treasury Department and named the US Life-Saving Service.

Sturgeon Point Lifesaving Station, Lake Huron, Michigan. The US Life-Saving Service built the station in Harrisville, Michigan, in 1876. The Sturgeon Point Life Boat Station became the Sturgeon Point Lifesaving Station. The volunteer crews stayed on duty until mid-December when navigation stopped for the winter season. In 1941, the Coast Guard closed the station and demolished the old boathouse. The lighthouse was closed but continued to operate as an aid to navigation. (Courtesy of the Don Bauman collection.)

East Tawas Lifesaving Station, Lake Huron, Michigan. This station was named Ottawa Point when it was first established in 1876. A complex set of stairs was used to get to the lookout tower. Soon the tower was removed and a new one constructed on the beach. The original station was abandoned, and a new one was built on the west side of the point. It is still in operation but is now known as East Tawas. A lifeboat crew is pictured here around 1918.

MICHIGAN CITY LIFESAVING STATION, LAKE MICHIGAN, INDIANA. In 1889, a new lifesaving station was built to monitor shipping and maritime need. Capt. Henry Finch led a meager but very competent six-man crew. In 1915, this station became part of the new US Coast Guard service. A new station was built in 1988.

MACKINAC ISLAND LIFESAVING STATION, STRAITS OF MACKINAC, MICHIGAN. The State Park Commission in 1915 provided waterfront property next to the Chippewa Hotel for a station. When it opened, it featured a first-floor boathouse with slips and a launching ramp for three small boats. The second floor had living quarters and a kitchen. The Coast Guard closed the Mackinac Island station in 1969, transferring operations to a new base in St. Ignace.

Erie Lifesaving Station, Lake Erie, Pennsylvania. Known as the Presque Isle Station when it was established in 1876, the station was moved from its original location in 1878 to a more advantageous site at Horseshoe Pond at the harbor's entrance.

Oswego Lifesaving Station, Lake Ontario, New York. In 1876, the Oswego station was commissioned on the west side of the harbor entrance. By 1877, a lifeboat station was also opened on the Salmon River and Sandy Creek. By 1967, the Oswego lights were automated.

Two Rivers Lifesaving Station, Lake Michigan, Wisconsin. The US Life-Saving Service came to the Two Rivers area in 1880. In 1908, the lifesaving station was relocated to its present site and officially became a Coast Guard station in 1915.

Rochester Lifesaving Station, Lake Ontario, New York, Pre-1907. Coast Guard Station Rochester is a part of the US Coast Guard's Ninth District and is manned year-round to provide assistance, search and rescue, and maritime security on Lake Ontario. Its area of responsibility reaches from Oak Orchard to Sodus Bay, New York, and out to the international border.

Resources

Brisson, Steven C. *Old Mackinac Point Lighthouse: A History and Pictorial Souvenir.* Mackinac Island, MI: Mackinac Island State Park, 2008.
Bryon, M. Christine, and Thomas R. Wilson. *Vintage Views of the Charlevoix-Petosky Region.* Petoskey, MI: Petoskey Co., 2005.
Edington, Richard F. *The Photographers Guide to Great Lakes Lighthouses.* Ashland, OH: Four Seasons Photography, 2009.
Encyclopedia Britannica.
Lighthouse Digest magazine.
www.lighthousefriends.com.
www.lighthousesofmichigan.com.
Michigan Lighthouse Conservancy.
Noble, Dr. Dennis L. *A Legacy: United States Life-Saving Service.* US Coast Guard Bicentennial Publications, 1987.
Pepper, Terry. *Lighting the Straits: Lighthouses of the Straits of Mackinac.* Mackinaw City, MI: Great Lakes Lighthouse Keepers Association, 2008.
Roach, Jerry. *The Ultimate Guide to Upper Michigan Lighthouses.* Durand, MI: Bug's Publishing, 2007.
Sapulski, Wayne S. *Lighthouses of Lake Michigan.* Manchester, MI: Wilderness Adventure Books, 2001.
The Great Lakes Lighthouse Keepers Association.
United States Coast Guard, US Department of Homeland Security.
www.us-lighthouses.com.
Wright, Larry, and Patricia Wright. *Great Lakes Lighthouses Encyclopedia.* Ontario, Canada: Boston Mills Press, 2006.

Discover Thousands of Local History Books Featuring Millions of Vintage Images

Arcadia Publishing, the leading local history publisher in the United States, is committed to making history accessible and meaningful through publishing books that celebrate and preserve the heritage of America's people and places.

Find more books like this at
www.arcadiapublishing.com

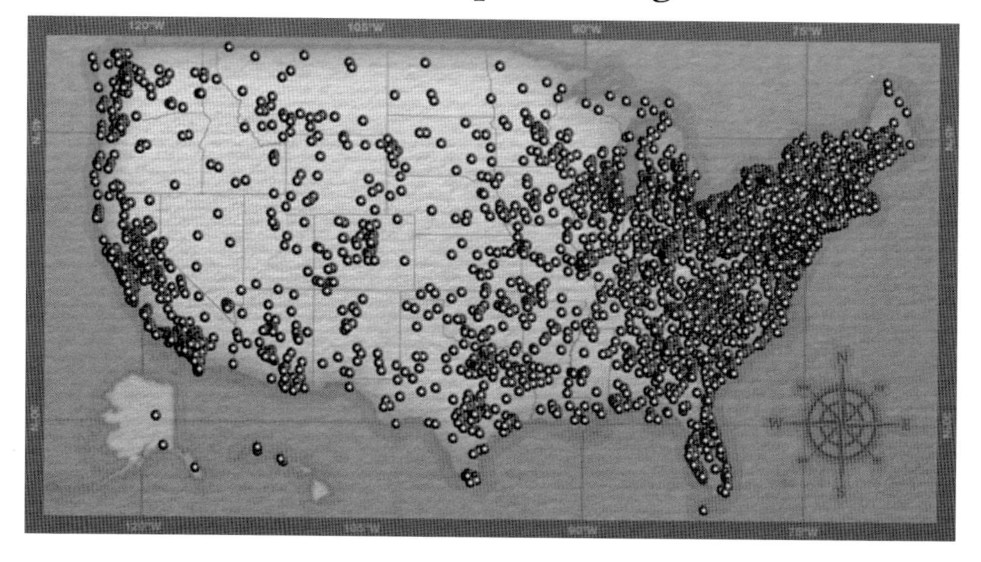

Search for your hometown history, your old stomping grounds, and even your favorite sports team.

Consistent with our mission to preserve history on a local level, this book was printed in South Carolina on American-made paper and manufactured entirely in the United States. Products carrying the accredited Forest Stewardship Council (FSC) label are printed on 100 percent FSC-certified paper.